DROPSHIPPING

E-COMMERCE BUSINESS

A Step by Step Guide for Beginners Who Want to Make
Money Online Selling on Amazon FBA, Shopify and
eBay. Create Your Passive Income and Find Your
Financial Freedom

Logan Brand

Table of Contents

Introduction

Thank you so much for downloading the book *Dropshipping e-commerce business: a step by step guide for beginners who want to make money online selling on Amazon FBA, Shopify and eBay. Create your passive income and find your financial freedom.*

As in this book, we will help you build your very own business, which will be very easy to manage.

Most of the information you have read or heard regarding dropshipping is very vague. In fact, most people don't know the actual methodology on how to start their dropshipping business without any hick-ups. Which is what we will be helping you with; we will teach you how to start your business and how to grow it to a very high-income generating asset.

Dropshipping can become a lucrative activity once you get to know the ins and outs of the business. While there isn't any complex science behind it, there are trade secrets that the leading players have been keeping to themselves. That is only natural. After all, would you share the secrets of your money-making machine with the world?

In this book, you will discover how the leading players in the business make their money. The best thing about it is that you will see that you don't need any specialized knowledge or advanced college degrees. All you need is to learn the inner workings of this business. Once you have figured out what's hiding under the hood, then you will be able to get started on your own.

It is simpler than you could have ever imagined it was. But you do need to know the secrets and methods that the leading players employ. Otherwise, you can give it the old college try, but you won't be as successful as you would like to be. As a matter of fact, that is where most folks attempt this business, but don't produce the results they would like. They end up falling short of their targets only to end up discouraged.

In this volume, we will not only talk about all of the top websites to drop-ship from, but we will also teach you how to market your business and how to make your dropshipping store a brand. Many people tend to sell products on their store to make a quick buck, but I am here to let you know a little secret—they don't make money. If you want to make money with dropshipping, you need to build a brand, which means that you will go into this business with a purpose. We will help you to find your purpose and your calling.

The most important thing to keep in mind is that becoming successful at dropshipping takes time and effort. While it would be nice to become rich overnight practically, this business takes time and practice before you can truly become good at it. As with anything in life, there is a learning curve. But fear not, this book aims to flatten that learning curve as much as possible. That way, your learning experience will be far easier and simpler than you would have otherwise experienced.

So, take the time to go through each of the chapters in the book thoroughly. Each section contains valuable insights that you will be hard-pressed to find readily available anywhere else. This way, the information presented in this book will be an entire reference library on the compiled subject in a single volume. That will make learning the dropshipping business seamless and straightforward.

So, it's time to roll up our sleeves and get started. We guarantee that you will be eager to get started running your own dropshipping business by the time you are done with the first couple of chapters of this book. Best of all, you have everything you need to get started.

We hope you enjoy the book. If you find it useful and informative, by all means, tell your friends, family and colleagues about it. They will certainly appreciate your interest in helping them learn about this potentially lucrative business.

Chapter 1:

What Is Dropshipping?

Ok, so now the big burning question is going to be answered. What is dropshipping? Well, simply put dropshipping is a business model where you are going to act as the "middle man."

So mostly what you are going to do is find a product from a supplier at a low price. After that is done, you will make an online store or sell on an online store, and regardless you will need a storefront from where you can sell and collect payments. Now the trick is to upload product photos and descriptions on your website, which most of the time your supplier will provide you with.

On your store or website, you will hike up the price of the product which you are getting really cheap, and finally, target it to specific groups of people who will be interested in purchasing your product.

Once they buy the product from you, then you will go to your supplier and buy it for a low price than what was offered and directly ship it to the buyer without you even touching the product, leaving you with some profit in your pocket.

Since you now know what dropshipping is, let me talk to you about the benefits of it compared to other business models. You see, there are a lot of benefits to doing a dropshipping style of business, and the main one is that you will not be holding any inventory. This means you won't have to make any significant upfront investments in buying a whole lot of products or renting out a warehouse where you can keep it. Another great benefit of this style of business model is that you will not have to worry about shipping the product; the supplier will take care of that for you.

To some, this might have been a shock. As some of us have grown to believe how to start your business, you need a significant upfront investment and a prominent storage place where you can keep all your products.

Well, I am here to tell you that those days are long gone.

The truth is that you don't need a whole lot of upfront investment to start your own business. All you need is a laptop or a computer, a high-quality product which you can get for cheap, a storefront with an audience. No significant upfront investment, no warehouse to rent, nothing. This is why dropshipping is one of the best business models of this day and age.

Now, there are two types of ways you can start your dropshipping business. Which we will go in-depth within this chapter, the first way is online dropshipping. This is the typical one, which is done by most people when they start their dropshipping business. The second one is warehouse dropshipping; although it requires a little more upfront investment, it still has a lot of benefits. That being said, let us dive deep into these two dropshipping methods.

Online Dropshipping

Online dropshipping is one of the most common ways people decide to start up their dropshipping business these days.

This is the method that comes to mind when people talk about dropshipping. With this, you will have to find a supplier who can provide you with high-quality products for a cheap price, one thing you have to make sure about is that he or she will have to ship out the product directly to the buyer, without you have to worry about that.

Using this method, you will most likely have to make your website using Shopify to make your online store or, if you don't want to create a website, you can use eBay. We will discuss more which sites to choose for your dropshipping business later in this book.

If you decide to use this method for your dropshipping, you will have to make sure that you have a safe and secure way of collecting payments from your client. Not only it will help you get paid safely, but it will also make your customers feel safe once they decide to purchase on your website or product.

If you are thinking about making a website for your products, then make sure you add a trust badge on your website. If you use Shopify as your dropshipping website, it will show a trust badge in the footer menu of your site. So, don't worry about that if you're considering using that side to create your dropshipping website.

One more thing to remember, make sure you have a PayPal account, most people will use it to make purchases on web sites. So if you want to get paid, create a PayPal account.

Benefits of using online dropshipping

I want to discuss the benefits of using online dropshipping for your business. Like I mentioned before, you don't have to hold any inventory, this means that you don't need to buy any products in bulk or rent out a warehouse where you can store your products. All you need is to make a website, upload the product on your site with markup, and once someone purchases the product, you will give the shipping information to your supplier, and he or she will mail it out to them. Plain and simple. The only thing you might need for the investment is to buy a domain name for your website, which I highly recommend. The domain would cost you around $10 a year. Also, if you don't do coding for a living, you might have to use a website platform to start selling your products and to collect payments which will cost you additionally $30 to $120 a month (depending on which website platform you decide to use, etc.) If you want, you can pay for the whole year with your website provider, which will save you money.

Just like any business model, there are some flaws in this method, so let's talk about them. The main one I see is shipping times, and we live in a world where websites ship products in a day. Most of the time, the supplier you will be working with would be from China, so the orders for your clients will be shipped out from China. To make a profit on your sale, you will have to use the most cost-efficient way of shipping, which will result in slower shipping times.

This isn't a total deal-breaker, but people are some more impatient than others. So if you don't pick the right supplier and shipping methods, you can expect to get refunds. Don't you worry, not all your orders will be refunded, and I will also show you the best tricks and techniques to get fast delivery to your client using this dropshipping method later in the book, but don't expect shipping times of a day like most big competitors offer as it won't be possible with this technique.

Another drawback or flaw with this business model is that you won't be able to tell the quality of the products, which you're going to be selling.

I would recommend you to buy the product before you put it up on your online store, it will reduce the risk that your products can be refunded for quality issues. One more thing you have to worry about is driving traffic to your product. Since you won't be affiliated with any big companies, you will have to drive traffic to your website or storefront using paid advertisements.

Warehouse Dropshipping

This method is similar to online dropshipping in some ways and different in others, let me explain.

This is identical in that no inventory is kept, and no products are shipped. Where it's different, compared to the online dropshipping method is that you will have to buy a certain amount of products upfront. However, the benefit of having products with you would be fast shipping, which will allow you to have fewer chances of refunds and have better customer satisfaction. So, let me explain to you how warehouse dropshipping work is precise.

The first thing to remember is that you will be selling your product on a website like Amazon. You can still use the warehouse dropshipping method with your website. Still, you will have to rent out a warehouse, and shipping would be your responsibility. Companies like Amazon will let you store it in their warehouse and ship the products out for you, which is why it is recommended to work with a big company when doing a warehouse dropshipping model. So how it works is: you find a product for cheap or buy it from a warehouse in bulk, and then you will ship your inventory to the company's warehouse.

Once that is done, you will sit back and see the profits in your bank account, and you don't have to worry about anything like customer service making a website or capturing a payment nothing. The company will take care of everything for you.

But, the upfront investment to start this business model is higher than the online dropshipping. Let me break it down for you.

Depending on the product and how much of it you buy, you are looking to spend $1,000 to $2,000 on your inventory. Companies also charge you to have a seller's account that will be around $39.99 or more depending on how many products you sell. Plasma fee for every product shipped.

So as you can see, there is quite a bit more upfront investment compared to the online dropshipping method. Although this method has a significant upfront investment, it also has some positives to consider.

Benefits of using warehouse dropshipping

There are a lot of benefits with this dropshipping method, so let us talk about them.

The best interest by using this dropshipping method is that you can actually quality check the products before you decide to sell your products. As you know by now, you must check the quality of your product before you ship them off for your refund rates to be lower.

Another great benefit with warehouse dropshipping is that, once you have shipped it to the warehouse companies, you don't have to worry about anything else. The company will take care of the shipping.

Another huge benefit of this business model is that you will not have to worry about your product's advertising as much as the online dropshipping method. Since your product will be listed on the website companies, which already gets a lot of traffic, you won't have to worry about promoting your product too much. That means fewer advertisements are paid and more money in your pocket.

All being said, there is one major flaw I see with this method of dropshipping. The flaw I see is that there is no guarantee that all your products will sell. Even though you will be listing your product on a website that gets a lot of traffic, it won't always equal to sales.

Remember, there will be a lot of products you will be competing with on the website, so making sure your product sells is crucial if you don't want to lose your investment.

So hopefully, you now know what dropshipping is and the different ways you can go about starting your dropshipping business. If you're still confused, then don't worry, keep reading, it will begin to get less confusing as we go along in this book.

Hopefully, everyone that had read this book now has an understanding of what it takes to start a dropshipping business. Trust me, dropshipping is one of the most straightforward business models to scale up and make money on, so keep on reading.

Chapter 2:

Start a Dropshipping Business

Now, you have an idea about the types of dropshipping business models and a rough idea on how to go about starting your own dropshipping business.

I would like to get into the specifics of starting your very own dropshipping business. If you have been doing some research online on dropshipping, you might have heard of a lot of websites on where you can start your business, but in this chapter, we will stick with the top three sites. Those three would be Shopify, Amazon, and eBay.

The reason why we will be only going through these websites is that every other dropshipping platforms are mimicking these three websites, so you don't need to worry about learning each dropshipping site, because they are similar to the top three. We will go into the details on each of the websites, and we will discuss things such as the exact start-up cost, how to get paid on and how many legs work will take to get started on each site. One more thing I would like to talk about is the income potential of each website, as there are a lot of misconceptions floating around the internet about this topic, so I will be covering that as well.

With that being said, let's start by going through the website, which popularized the whole dropshipping business model, which is Shopify.

Shopify

For people who don't know what Shopify is, it is an e-commerce company founded in Canada.

What Shopify provides is an e-commerce platform or an online store for its users; it was initially founded by

Scott Lake, Daniel Weingard, and the current CEO Tobias Lutke. Essentially, Shopify provides you with a secure online store where you can sell your products to the costumers. Most people use this website for online dropshipping rather than warehouse dropshipping since Shopify does not provide users with a warehouse. That being said, starting your very own dropshipping business using Shopify as your platform is straightforward and cost-effective compared to other platforms.

To start making money using Shopify as your platform, you will need a supplier, which can ship out the products anywhere in the world for a lower price. That is for the requirements.

I want to get specific with a start-up cost of getting started with Shopify as it is not free, but it is cost-efficient compared to other business models out there.

First, you will need to buy a domain name. You need to make sure that your website looks legit, and for that reason, you will need the domain name. Purchasing a domain name is inexpensive, it will only cost you around $11 in a year, depending on the domain name.

Once you get that sorted, you will have to sign up on Shopify. Since Shopify offers a free 14-day trial, I recommend that you assure that the store name or brand you come up with is not taken before you buy any domain name for your website or store.

Once you have decided your store name, it will be the time to buy a package from Shopify, which will allow you to start selling your products. Shopify offers three packages, which include:

- Basic Shopify package = USD 29/mth
- Shopify package = USD 79/mth
- Advanced Shopify package = USD 299/mth

Also, note if you want to save money. You can buy these packages every year. But that's totally up to you.

You might be wondering which one to get started with? Well, let me explain each of them to you.

If you're beginning your dropshipping business, I would say that you don't need the advanced Shopify package.

Once you have your business rolling and if you want to expand it, you can do your research on it and upgrade, but for starters, pick between the Basic Shopify package and the Shopify package. If your funds are low, and you want to start making money online, then you can start with the basic package. Still, if you have some extra cash to spare, then I would recommend upgrading to the Shopify package as it has some useful benefits.

The useful benefits this Shopify package provides you, compared to the Basic Shopify package, is the lower amount of online credit card rates compared to the Basic Shopify package. Even though it's minuscule, it adds up once you start making over thousands of dollars a month. Another great benefit of using the Shopify package compared to the Basic Shopify package is that you can start making your gift cards; as you know, to make sales on this platform, you will need to get some traffic first before you can make some sales online.

So having these small incentives can add more purchases in the future. Other than that, these packages are identical; if you are using Shopify for online dropshipping purposes, you can go with either package which fits your budget. Now it's up to you which one you want to get started.

One more thing, you can invest in making your store stand out, are the logos, you will need a logo for your Shopify store. You can get it done professionally by hiring someone on fiverr.com, and that will not cost you more than USD 25 to get started.

One thing you must note: you do not need to hire someone to make your logo; it can be quickly done for free by using canva.com. But whether it is free or not, you will need a logo.

How Much It Cost?

To sum, up the total costs of getting started with dropshipping using Shopify:

- Shopify package $29or $79
- Domain name $ 11 to $18
- Logo $0.00 to $25

So, to get started with Shopify, it will cost you $40+ $29 every month, if you choose the cheapest option, or $122+ $79every month. Regardless the start-up should be quite affordable for anyone.

How Work On It?

Now, let's talk about the work you will have to make for your Shopify business to flourish. You will have to make sure your website looks presentable. For that, Shopify provides you with some great themes which can be used to build your website with no problems. But it does require some work to be put in.

Another thing you will have to take care of is customer inquiries and complaints. Since it is your brand and company, you will have to deal with everything from claims to fulfilling an order. So make sure you have an e-mail created for your store inquiries, also, as I said before, you will have to emphasize more on getting traffic because no one would know your store, except for your family and friends. Other than that, you should be fine.

How you get paid on Shopify is simple as well; all you need is to make a PayPal account because some people might choose PayPal to complete their transaction. Also, Shopify will ask your banking information, for the ones who want to use a credit card to purchase on your store. Then Shopify can directly deposit into your account.

The final point I would like to discuss is how much you can earn using Shopify and the online dropshipping method. Since it is your brand and your company, you can make as much as you want. You can become a millionaire or a billionaire with this method, as long as you build a following for your business, which again will be talked about in the next chapters. Overall the sky is the limit. Work hard and be patient—you will get what you desire.

Amazon FBA

Amazon is one of the largest e-commerce companies in the world, and its founder and owner's net worth is $150 billion, making him the richest man in the world. Jeff Bezos founded his company in the early 90s, and his goal was to sell books online. Now, Amazon sells everything you can imagine.

Amazon is the biggest e-commerce company in the world, and its website has one of the highest amounts of online traffic in the world, needless to say, working with Amazon could make you money.

Now you might be wondering, what does the FBA stand for? It stands for fulfillment by Amazon.

What you have to do to be a part of this program is simple. First, find a product which you can get for cheap, second buy them in bulk, and finally, the third step is to ship it to Amazon warehouse where it can be shipped off to the customer.

How Much It Cost?

It is simple, now the start-up cost with this business model is a little bit higher, so let's break it down:

- Buying products in bulk for cheap $1000 - $ 3000
- If you sell more than 40 items a month, you will have to pay $39.99

At the lower end, you can get started from USD 1000 to USD 3000, plus an additional $39.99 a month if you sell more than 40 products. Plus, there is a charge for each product they ship out, but don't worry, it will only be charged once someone orders a product.

Even though there is a significant upfront investment in this type of dropshipping, it still has some benefits; for example, your products will be listed on Amazon, and you will already be getting free traffic, which would equal higher chances of a sale. Unlike Shopify, Amazon takes care of the back ends like customer refunds, questions, etc. All you do is get the product, ship it to Amazon's warehouse, and you will start earning money.

How Work on It?

Now let's talk about the work you will have to do to get this business started from the ground up.

The first thing you have to do is find a cheap supplier, to make some profits; you will have to find products at a cost. Second, buy it in bulk, and third, ship it to Amazon's warehouse.

When a business takes off, all you have to worry about is restocking your products by shipping it to Amazon, so you can make more money, that's all the work you will have to. As I said, Amazon would take care of all the back end stuff such as shipping, customer service, etc.

Let's talk about how you will get paid on Amazon FBA; it is merely similar to Shopify.

First, you have to make a seller account on Amazon; once that is done, you will add your banking information to the account. Amazon will pay you the profits you made right into your bank account, and you don't have to worry about anything else, besides filing your taxes.

The final thing I would like to talk about income is how much can you make on Amazon FBA.

Since Amazon FBA is not a personal brand, which you can grow, the revenue will be limited. I know the top earners can make over two million a year using Amazon

FBA. This, for some people, can be amazing to see this amount of cash. But for others who want to build their brand, Amazon FBA would not be the answer. Now the benefit with this business model is that if you do everything right, you can make money faster and scale up to higher, but there is a tap on the amount of money you can make here.

eBay

eBay is one of the most successful e-commerce websites, founded in 1995 by Pierre Omidyar.

It became quickly in a recognized household name around the world, what started as a bidding website online has now become one of the most popular places to sell your items, and it also can be used with great success for drop-shippers all around the world.

Now, starting up with eBay as a drop-shipper would probably be the cheapest way to go.

To get started, all you will need a supplier who can provide you with competitive products and a PayPal account to accept payments.

How Much It Cost?

There are no upfront costs to get started, and you can use the supplier's images have on their page, and upload it to your eBay account. The way eBay makes money is through transactions. Once someone purchases a product from you, eBay will take a cut out of that purchase, plain and simple. So to get started with eBay, you will need $0 and a cheap connection for your products.

How Work on It?

I know, eBay sounds like the best option out of the three right now, but there are some significant flaws.

The first one is you can't build a brand as you could do on Shopify, and you see what appeals to most people is trying out a new brand and see what they like. With eBay, it's like buying something for really cheap and on sale, so it would be hard to mark up your products at a larger scale like you could on Amazon and Shopify, which would equal fewer profits.

Another problem I see with this method is that it is competing with Amazon, which already has a more significant following and is more trusted by people. So with that in mind, getting organic traffic as you would on Amazon would be hard.

I would recommend spending some money on ads if you want to get sales on eBay since the competition is so high it will make it hard for your product to sell organically.

With all being said, let's talk about how you will be paid on eBay. Like the other websites, you will be paid through PayPal, so make sure you have your PayPal account set up. But don't forget eBay will take some money out of the transaction online, and so will PayPal.

So keep that in mind as you move forward. For all that wants to get started on eBay don't worry, as there is some money to be made. eBay drop-shippers can make $1,000 to $ 3,000 as a side income every month, which isn't bad at all, but you can't expect to become a millionaire through eBay. So if you are looking to make a side income, then eBay can defiantly fulfill that for you for with no start-up cost.

Now, it's your choice to pick out which website and dropshipping method you want to work with to start your own dropshipping business.

I know that all of these websites have some fantastic benefits, but they also come with some issues. Finding which type of dropshipping business you need to start is simple. First, ask yourself how much money can you invest; second, ask yourself how much money do you want to make; and third, how much of that income do you want it to be passive, meaning you don't do a lot of work, and you earn profits.

If you have money to invest and want to see quick returns and passive, then Amazon FBA would be the right fit for you. If your goal is to start your own company and build your brand while making incredible amounts of money, then Shopify would be the answer for you.

Finally, if you want to make money but you don't have money to invest, then I would highly recommend eBay so you can start earning some side income quickly.

I hope this chapter opened your mind to the different ideas of dropshipping. As I said, it is up to you to decide on picking the right business model for your needs.

It is time for you to evaluate your situation and come up with a business plan that works for you. All three websites can make you earn money. Some more than the others, but again, there is a price to pay at each site, so choose wisely.

Chapter 3:

Most Profitable Niche

In this chapter, we will talk about the niche and how to find the right niche for you when it comes to dropshipping.

Many people don't realize that, but the niche that you pick will dictate how well your store is going to do in regards to the sale and how successful it is going to be when it comes to overall brand awareness. In this book, we're not just going to talk about finding a profitable niche and making it marketable. We will talk about how to start a dropshipping store that you can make money from and turn it into a brand. You must think like that when you are starting a dropshipping business, as many people are beginning to feel like they need to pick a niche and advertise it on Facebook, and they will see the results which they are hoping for. But I'll be the first one to tell you that this isn't true at all, that being said, you need to understand what niche you're going to be getting into, and why you must pick out the right one. We will break it down for you to have a clear idea of the niche you're going to be working on starting your very own dropshipping store.

What Is a Niche?

Now before we dive deep into this topic, let's talk about the niche and what it entails. Niche is essential; this a way of saying that a specific type of people like a particular type of product. For example, if you are selling dog products, then you are in the dog niche, as you are attracting customers who have a dog and would like to buy products for them. In essence, this is a niche.

Now that you're fully aware of what a niche is, let's talk about how to start your very own dropshipping business the right way by picking out the right niche.

Don't Experiment

One of the best advices you will ever get when it comes to picking out a niche would be not to experiment. The reason why I recommend you not to test is because many people would experiment and get into a niche that they don't know about, and then they will fall and tumble.

The truth is that you need to pick out a niche that you are well-versed in. For example, if you are very passionate about health and wellness, then it has advised that you pick out your brand based on Health and Wellness. Don't go into selling dog products if you don't know anything about dogs, stick with the niche that you know about.

Sometimes the niche that you're in will not be as profitable as you think it is, which is fine, there are also some things called a sub-niche.

You can get into it and easily find a profitable niche, in which you know the right amount about and can start selling products. For instance, we would never recommend that you begin a dropshipping store based on Amazon's platform.

We would not recommend you start a general store; the reason why it is not advised for you to start one is that many people are already doing it and they are dominating. For example, Amazon is already dominating the general niche store, which is why if you step into this broad niche, you will not see the success you have been looking for, especially in the long-term.

You might see some progress in the beginning. However, it will be tough for you to keep it up for a sustained amount of time.

On the other hand, when it comes to finding something nice that you really love and finding products that you know, people who share the same interests as you would like you, and you will be in a much better position when it comes to selling product and gaining a new customer.

Moreover, I highly recommend that you pick a niche that you have extreme amounts of knowledge in; if you can find any and sell the products at the same time and your dropshipping store, then you will be in a prime position to making it a very successful brand.

So, to sum it up, if you do some research online and find a very profitable niche in your forte when it comes to knowledge, then we would highly recommend that you use that niche to make it a brand.

However, we do not recommend that you start selling products and make a brand of a niche that you don't know anything about but is profitable, because it will not make you earn a lot of money in the long term.

One thing to remember is that clients look for people who genuinely are invested in their brand, and the brand owner should know a lot about the products that they are selling. Consumers are astute, which is why you must know what you're selling and have a passion for it.

How to Find a Niche?

Now that you've understood how to pick a niche, let's talk about how to find a profitable niche.

Much of the time, it is tough to find a niche that you know is going to be useful, which is why we recommend a simple process to find out which niche is profitable. For example, one of the best ways to find out if a niche is going to be useful is to go on Amazon.

Many people believe that Amazon is a Google search for consumer habits, merely going to the best-seller's product and see which one is selling at the top.

If the products are selling very well on Amazon, then the chances you can mimic the sales volume as well to a certain degree. The best-case scenario for you would be going to Amazon and look at the niche which you're trying to get into.

Go to Amazon and search up health and fitness, if that's the niche you know right. Look at all the top-selling products. If you find that yoga mats which have a good selling on Amazon, means that their Amazon best-seller rank is less than 50,000, then it is possible for you to turn that yoga mat into a brand.

Based on your dropshipping store on those yoga mats, it has been done a million times and has yielded success on the drop-shippers.

One thing you have to remember is that you will not be able to keep up with Amazon prices. Many people who sell on Amazon cut their profits to a minimum, and this will not be possible for you. To see amazing results from your dropshipping business, you will have to make sure that you turn your store into a brand that people can start loving. We will talk about how to build up a brand later in this book, but one thing you need to realize when it comes to finding a niche and making it a brand is that you need to make a product or a culture that people can love.

Once people start enjoying the lifestyle, the sales will come pouring in. Which is why it is essential to understand how to build up a brand, your main goal is to find people who love the culture of your brand and once you find those people you will see the money coming in. Moreover, once you've managed to find people who love your brand, then they will not hesitate to pay more than what they get on Amazon for the same product. Marketing is the key, which is why finding a niche and what you love is very important.

To sum up, let's talk about how to find a profitable niche in the correct way.

The first thing you need to do is follow the Amazon blueprint we just spoke about, meaning we want you to go on Amazon and look up all the products in your niche.

Once you have done that narrow down all the products which have a best-seller rank of less than 50,000, these are your winner products which you can base your brand on.

The second way to find out if your niche is profitable is going on Google Trends and look up the products which you are interested in selling, this is a good way to know. You will find out when your selected products were trending, and when they were not trending on Google, this will give you a great idea of where you are standing. This stuff isn't as crucial as the Amazons.

However, it is important to find out if the product is going to be a winner or if people are actively looking for it. The final way to know if the product is going to be profitable or if you found a profitable niche is to look at all the Instagram and Facebook pages. You can find a ton of Instagram and Facebook pages dedicated to that brand with the product that you are trying to sell. Then you will be in a good position to find out if you are going to make it in the dropshipping business. With more popularity comes a lot more competition, which is what we're going to be talking about now.

How to Fight Off Competition in Your Niche?

Once you have figured out which niche you're going to be starting your dropshipping business in, It is now time for you to weed out all the competition and come up with a game plan. In popular niches, there's a lot of competition, which is why you need to figure out a way to fight off the competition. One of the ways to fight off competition in a niche is by offering a lower price.

However, we believe this isn't the way you should be going about it. One of the best ways to fight off competition in your niche is by having a better culture and a product that has never been sold before or marketed in a way it should have.

It is not that difficult to find innovative products from Chinese wholesalers, which is why we advise you to keep doing your research and keep going about finding a way to sell your product. This would mean for you to bring up amazing facts about those products that you're going to be promoting.

For example, if you're looking to sell yoga mats on your dropshipping store, then I highly recommend that you sell it in a way where people not only can feel rejuvenated by the information you provided but feel good about the purchase. You can say the yoga mat is made from reusable plastic. Many people care about the environment in the health and fitness industry, and this would mean that it would be an excellent idea for you to market it as such. This is hypothetically speaking, and we recommend that you come up with your brand awareness and your brand model.

Another way to fight off competition in your niche would be not only selling products that are innovative but also to offer subscription-based products. In today's world, subscription-based products work very well. So, to ride this horse quickly would be an excellent benefit for your brand.

This would also mean that you will be getting reoccurring sales more frequently, and your sales and revenue will remain pretty much stable. Stability is the key when it comes to dropshipping, and this would be a good idea for you to start to have products that you can turn into a subscription base or counter them with a better deal.

Facebook Groups and Instagram Pages

This is another place where you can find niches to sell. A lot of Facebook and Instagram pages are made for sharing videos and contents online for people to look at simply because they are big fans. They have a special connection to this niche for some reason, and it could be a person who knows about it. But you can use this fan page or groups to offer them something they can't refuse.

Think about it, if you were a big fan of dogs and you love dogs. Wouldn't you want to buy a $25 T-shirt which says I love dogs? Of course, you would because you are a super-fan.

Now, the best part about this method is that the people you will advertise your product most likely will buy it. There are a lot of pages online where there is a big following but no products to sell.

So, to find these pages, all you will have to do is search and think outside the box, as some pages are perfect for selling—I love "something" T-shirt. Look around and explore, and once you find your niche, you will make some serious profits.

With all that being said, let me share with you some niches that made me have money in the past, keep in mind that these niches have been proven to make money. But like we told you previously, if you have no interest in this niche, then it is best advised that you do not dabble with them. Use the techniques provided in this book to find a niche that helps you to make a brand with a motto that sells and attracts a specific type of people. Please don't forget it.

Here are the top 5 niches we believe have great potential:

- Dog lovers
- Cat lovers
- Health and wellness
- Car lovers
- Electronic accessories

These niches are still quite profitable, so do your research, and if you like, sell based on these.

To finish off this chapter, I would like to remind you how essential findings the right niche is. A niche will either do your business or break it, so if you don't do your research before you decide to sell your products online, then you will regret it. Make sure you use the techniques I taught to find the right niches to sell on and, also, feel free to use the niche I have personally made money on, maybe it could make you some money with them as well. Now, go online and start researching and find the niche you will be selling on.

Chapter 4:

Finding Suppliers or Wholesalers

Finding the right supplier or the right wholesalers for your dropshipping business is imperative, meaning that you can't "cheap out" or not care about this aspect.

As you can imagine, your business will revolve around your supplier quite a bit. Truth be told, if you don't have any products that you can sell, then it would honestly be impossible for you to make any money, which would equal to no profits.

On the other hand, if you decide to "cheap out" and sell low-quality products, chances are people will return the products, even though we discussed the importance of finding a proper niche to the importance of advertising the product the right way. It can't be overridden by an unreliable or a cheap, low-quality product.

Finding the right supplier for your dropshipping business is imperative, for both quality purposes and shipping purposes.

If you are going to be using Amazon FBA or a similar type of dropshipping method, then shipping times do matter for you to stock up your products, but it isn't the biggest of the deal for that dropshipping model compared to the Shopify methods. With all that being said, quality is the most significant factor you have to worry about when selling your products.

Now, we will go through the top websites from where you can find great suppliers for your business, we will also talk about how to build a great relationship with them. Finally, for everyone dropshipping using the method online-drop shipping, I will reveal a secret to getting the fastest shipping anywhere in the world, so your customers stay happy and fewer refunds are being made.

We will break this chapter into two phases.

First, we will talk about how to find suppliers for people using online dropshipping. We will go through everything from finding the product, building a relationship with the seller, getting it shipped fast, and of course, making sure the product is of high quality.

Then we will talk about finding a supplier or a whole-seller for the warehouse dropshipping method, so with that being said, we'll start with online dropshipping.

Suppliers For Online Dropshipping

Finding a supplier for people using online dropshipping for a business model could be challenging.

Since most of the time, you will be going by assumptions, what our job with this process is to take out as much of the guesswork as we can and find the winning supplier which we are looking for.

Now, there are a lot of websites online where you can find products for cheap. But from my experience AliExpress has one of the best quality products and shipping times, if you have been doing some research online, you might have heard things like "AliExpress is dead" or things of that nature. But I am here to tell you that AliExpress still works amazingly and will help you make some serious profits online.

There are some tips and techniques you need to know before you fully start using AliExpress as your sole supplier.

Now, if you don't know what AliExpress is, then let me clarify it for you: Think of AliExpress like the Amazon of China. There are a lot of people selling products online on this website, mostly from China, and as we know, most of the products are manufactured in China, meaning the mark upon the products would be a lot less.

You can quickly sell it online for a higher price in the North American market, and to make things even better, the products on AliExpress are mostly similar types of products that are sold or are popular in the North American market. These people selling on AliExpress are selling it to people specifically who want to start their dropshipping business.

There are some guidelines you need to follow before you start to use AliExpress to drop-ship products from, as there are some flaws. The things we need to look into before we start selling products using AliExpress are these:

- Suppliers review
- Product photos and description
- E-packet
- How many orders sold

If all these points check out, then your supplier is right. So let's begin with the supplier review. To find out if the supplier is correct, the first thing you will need to do is check the reviews, make sure the review on his or her store is at least 95% positive. If that's not the case, then either the quality of the product isn't right or the product is something else when it gets delivered.

Another thing to worry about is photos and the description. If the product has excellent photos and description, then most of the time, it shows that the seller cares about what he or she is doing and will do whatever it takes to keep his customers happy.

It is important to take care of shipping because if the seller offers a shipping method known as e-packet, then the shipping times would be a lot faster than other suppliers. Usually, e-packet delivers the product in 2-3 weeks, which is the fastest shipping times you will get on AliExpress, so make sure your supplier provides you with an e-packet.

Also, to make sure this supplier is reliable, check out how many orders he/she has had, if it is higher than 500 orders, then they are in the clear. If all the points I just described to you have all of these characteristics, then the supplier is the right supplier, and you can indeed start to grow your business with him or her. If the supplier doesn't check out on all these points, then you have to find a new one.

The Vendor

After the manufacturer, the next dropshipping supply chain entity is known as the vendor.

The vendor is the point in the supply chain that will sell the products that the manufacturer has made to large retail stores to make a profit. To make that profit, the vendor will need to raise the price of the product when they sell it to a retail store.

Still, it's not recommended that you look at your dropshipping business as being able to compete at the vendor level, at least not on its onset. The amount of product that these vendors are ready to sell is quite large, and many times these vendors will even have contracts with the companies to whom they're selling. Unless you already have contacts that will be able to procure you these types of deals, being a vendor is also not in your best interest.

The Seller

Since you're most likely not going to be the manufacturer or the vendor, the place that your business will probably fit best is within the seller portion of the supply chain. The seller can be best described as an individual or small business that purchases the product from the vendor. The seller makes his or her profit by making sure that the price at which they're selling the product to their customers is higher than the rate at which they bought it.

This is an important concept that you need to understand regarding developing an online dropshipping business because if you end up selling your products at a price similar to or lower than the price at which you bought the product yourself, you will not make any good profit.

A typical percentage that can be used when you're considering how much you want to increase the price of a product is either 1.5 or 1.6%. Of course, you can adjust this percentage as it fits into your business.

Negotiating With Manufacturers, Vendors and Other Sellers

As you should be able to see from the description of each aspect of the supply chain above, you—the dropshipping entities—are going to exist within the selling portion of the supply chain model.

However, this does not mean that the potential does not exist to interact with all three of these dropshipping entities along the supply chain in some manner.

A vital aspect of any dropshipping business is figuring out which manufacturers and vendors will agree to ship their products to your customers on your behalf. In other words, instead of having a manufacturer or a vendor send their products to you so that you can then send it to your customer, some manufacturers and vendors will agree to ship to other people for you, free of charge. Dropshipping is not just a product-focused business because the customer is going to go through your dropshipping business. It essentially means that he or she does not have to interact with a large and sometimes-overwhelmingly slow manufacturer.

This positions the dropshipper as a business that is merely serving as a point of contact for a customer so that he or she does not have to go through the manufacturer or the vendor. With this being the case, it's essential to understand that any dropshipping business is a service, rather than an operation that buys and then re-sells products.

Without having excellent customer service, even a reputable drop shipping service is likely to go out of business! It's essential to keep this in mind because excellent client communication is a crucial element of any good dropshipping business.

Ali Pocket

One more tip I would share with you is that AliExpress tends to take some time when processing a payment. It could take up to three days, and it is done simply for their security. If you want to expedite the payment process for your order to be shipped faster, then I would recommend using Ali Pocket. Ali Pocket is similar to a gift card. It is like a safe credit card for AliExpress. So if you buy Ali Pocket in bulk and use it to purchase the product which you will be shipping it out to your client, then there would be no time to waste for processing a payment and the order would be shipped right away.

Print on demand

AliExpress is excellent for selling new trending stuff. But if your goal is to sell fan t-shirts or some like that, it might not be the right choice for you.

AliExpress has a lot of things to sell online, but the products it sells are not specific to niches and people. This is where print on demand t-shirts come in.

What is print on demand? It is a service where you come up with a logo. Pick out a t-shirt, sweater or whatever they have. Then what will happen is that the company will use your logo put it on a t-shirt and directly ship it out to the customer or the buyer.

There are a lot of websites to choose from. But the one I highly recommend is <u>Pillow profits</u>. It is fantastic not only do they have your good old t-shirts but they also offer things like pillowcases, shower curtain bed sheets which can be sent to a customer with your logo on any of those things.

Print on demand is ideal for those super niche fan pages we talked about before, since those fan pages are unique and hard to find you need to be unique with your products just like the page you are promoting it to.

So, if your store is based on super-niche products, then it would be hard to find products on AliExpress, and this is where print on demand comes in.

What print on demand will offer you this, cheap supplies with whatever you want on it and fast shipping? Most of the print on demand websites has a speedy delivery since most of them are based in out of the United States, so you don't need to worry about shipping or any of that make sure to pick out a print on demand website you like and come up with a logo.

Building Relationships With Your Suppliers

Let's talk about building relationships with your suppliers, and you must create a great relationship with your supplier. Not only will it help you make more profits, but it will also help you get faster shipping times. What I am going to tell you about applies more to AliExpress rather than print on demand websites. Regardless of which site it is, you need to have a great relationship with your supplier. So, to build good relationships with them, here are the ways you can do it:

- Give them business
- Be accepting
- Leave them great review's

Giving them business is quite self-explanatory. If you want to build a great relationship, you have to provide them with a company, and you can't expect to be their "special customer" if you don't buy anything from them. So make sure you first buy at least 20-25 items before you can think about asking them for a discount on your products.

Another thing to be mindful of is making sure you don't get angry at them for a shipment, which is a couple of days after or things of that nature. You have to remember they are trying their best to keep you happy, just like you do with your customers. The final word is to leave a positive review because, let's face it, everyone cares about positive reviews.

If you follow all these steps, you will start to build a great relationship with your supplier, and you can slowly begin to ask for things like discounts on your orders, which would mean a higher profit margin for you. So make sure you begin to build a great relationship with them.

With all that said, that was for finding a supplier for people using online dropshipping. Now, let's talk about finding suppliers for people using Amazon FBA or warehouse dropshipping. It is a little bit different but shares some of the same principles.

Suppliers for Warehouse Dropshipping

To find suppliers or products for this type of dropshipping is a little bit easier compared to online dropshipping. Since you can inspect all the product before you start selling, makes it one step easier compared to the others. So, in short, there are three ways you can go about finding a supplier. The first one is using sites like Ali express, the second one is to find a warehouse where they are selling the products for cheap, and finally, buy products on exclusive sales and re-sell them.

Now, you already know how to find the right supplier on AliExpress, but let us talk about how you can use AliExpress as a warehouse dropshipping.

So right of the bat, once you find a product that you would like to sell, I would highly recommend you to buy one and check its quality. Once you have checked it out and made sure that the quality is of a high caliber, then you should contact the supplier and work out a deal.

You see, since you will be buying the product in bulk, there would be higher chances of you getting it for a further discounted price, so make sure you ask for it so you can make even more profit. Finally, once that is all done, ship it to the warehouse and start selling.

That was using AliExpress, now let's talk about using a warehouse or an exclusives sale to find your supplies. People don't realize that there are a lot of warehouses like Costco, where you can buy stuff for cheap and sell it on Amazon.

The way these process works is simple. Go to a warehouse-like Costco, search the product in bulk for a low price, and then transport it to Amazon's warehouse and start selling.

Trust me, I have seen so many affordable products on Costco for sale, which have made me some enormous profits. Make sure you find these products and start selling them on Amazon.

One of the ways I have made tremendous amounts of money on Amazon FBA is by waiting for sales like Black Friday or something like that. I would buy products on sale for 50% to even 70% off, and after the deal is made, I would sell it on Amazon at its original price.

Although this method is not as frequently occurring as the other two, it will yield you a lot of profits, so make sure you wait for these sales to make some real cash.

Finally, one secret method I have used before is finding listings on craigslist and Facebook market places for products and supplies.

Most of the time, you will find brand new stuff for sale near you, and the seller would be selling it off for next to nothing. So this would be your time to shine, find something in bulk for really cheap on these websites, work out a deal and sell it off on Amazon for an enormous profit.

If you found something inexpensive, but the quantity is low, then I would recommend using eBay to sell it on. I remember seeing a brand new iPhone very cheap, so just like anyone else would do; I bought it and sold it off on eBay for a significant profit.

Whatever you can find on these websites for a cheap price, make sure to act on them as soon as possible before they are gone.

To conclude this chapter, I would like to remind you how important it is to have the right supplier. This one can either do your business or break it, making sure you have the right supplier is imperative as it will only help you have a longer sustained activity.

So please, make sure you read this chapter very carefully, practice all the tricks and techniques taught in this chapter to find the right provider. Don't settle for a product or supplier which "gets the job done" if you want your business to be the best it can then find a product or a supplier which would be the best you can find in terms of service quality, and of course price.

Also, don't forget to keep your suppliers happy. Like I said, if you want to get better deals on your products, you need to make sure your relationship with your supplier is excellent.

Chapter 5:

Finding a Highly Profitable Product

Finding the right product is very crucial when it comes to dropshipping. We have briefly talked about how to find a product that will sell very well in your niche.

However, we will get very specific in this chapter as we will give you the tricks and tips on how to find a profitable product that can make you hundreds of thousands of dollars. This will only work if you have a great idea on how to market your product appropriately, we will talk about marketing the right way soon; however, it is crucial for you to find a product that can be sold.

That being said, we will make it very easy for you in terms of finding a product that can be sold. We will give you tried-and-true methods which will help you to not only find a product which will make you a lot of money, but you can scale and build a brand on. We keep talking about building a brand when it comes to dropshipping, as you must create a brand if your goal is to make a lot of money in the long term.

Nonetheless, finding a product of high quality and delivered it quickly is essential when it comes to dropshipping, the truth is that many people who dropship take a long time to get the product to the customers. This is not the ideal case scenario, which is why we also recommend that you find a product that has excellent shipping rates and also, excellent quality.

One of the ways to test out if the product is built in high quality is by buying the product and do all the things that are supposed to do.

This concept is very important. Make sure that all the products that you sell in your store are of high quality. This will put you in a position where you will be a step ahead of all your competition. At the end of the day, we want to be successful in the niche we're going to be in, so it is also essential that you sell better products than your competitors.

Finding those products isn't as hard as you think it is. There is a lot of trial and error when you have to find a product that will sell in your niche. With that being said, let's talk about some of the ways that many successful dropshippers use to find out if the product is going to be of good quality.

Finding Good Quality Products

The first topic we are going to be talking about is up to quality, finding high-quality products will help you to scale it up and to have more returning customers.

Many of the top brands like Nike get most of their sales from returning customers. This is why you must find products that will help you get more returning customers because from here is where the majority of your sales will come from.

The reason why the customers will return to your brand is that many people who genuinely believe in it and the product that you're selling. It comes to building up your clientele base, and this will only come if you are providing your customers with a quality product.

One of the many ways to find if the product is going to be quality or not is going to the dropshipping suppliers from AliExpress and read the reviews.

Believe it or not, the reviews on AliExpress are quite genuine, and they can help you tremendously when it comes to finding out if the product is going to be more successful in the long-term and how the quality is.

Read the review on AliExpress to find out if a product is of excellent quality. Most of the time, dropshippers have written the reviews, so you know who will be reliable. Once you've read the reviews and think that you can sell the product in your niche, buy the product. Feel out the product and see if it is durable and made out of good quality.

Figure out if the product is excellent, then you can go ahead and start selling it in your store. The only way to know if the product is right is to buy the product.

I know you will have to spend a little bit of money to get it to your house, but it is highly advised that you buy the product before you start selling. This will not only give you a better understanding of how the product is and works, but it would also help you understand if the product worth the money or not to your consumers.

Finding a Trending Product

The next thing we are going to be talking about is how to find a trending product and also help you to get more sales.

The beautiful thing when you are searching for a product, it's finding out if people need it. Most of the time, people are impulse buyers, especially on Facebook and Instagram. So, it is advised that you find a product that is not only trending, but it is in your niche.

Facebook

What is the best place to find a trending product and make a lot of money? Look up on Facebook by typing in "shop now."Keywords will give you a great idea of who are advertising the products, and how well the products are positioned. Looking at other people's ads will provide you with a better idea if the product is worth selling or not. Many dropshippers who are making millions of dollars use the SEC (Company Search Page) to find products that will sell. This is why it is highly advised that you find products through this method. It's just fine simply keeping looking for products, and eventually, to find a product with a good ad copy and good sales pitch, which has more than 50,000 views on Facebook. Then you will be in better hands to find a product which will help you to figure out if this worth to be sold online and in your store.

Amazon

That being said, another way to find a trending product is to look up on Amazon.

As we told you previously, people who sell on Amazon are merely selling them because it is working. This means it is one of the best ways to figure out if a product is going to make you a lot of money or not.

Look at the best-seller rank on Amazon. If the best seller rank is below 50,000, then you have found your winning product. However, when you're doing this test on Amazon, make sure that you pick out the niche your store is based on. If you search "best sellers,"you may not find a product that is based on your niche. The truth is that there is millions of merchandise ready to sell in your niche, so make sure that you only look for products in best-sellers when you are searching on Amazon.

eBay

Another way to find out if the product is trending is to go on eBay. Many people tend to not check up on eBay to find products, but the truth is that eBay is one of the best sources to find out if the product is going to be hot or not and look at all the best sellers in your niche on eBay. Many people make money dropshipping on eBay, so we advise you to find products on eBay which are already selling pretty good and that you can transfer it into your website. The final way to find out a trending product that helps you to make a lot of money in your store is the Google search in all the new trends.

Google Trends

As you know, Google Trends is one of your best friends when we talk about dropshipping. You can look up product names on Google Trends, and it will tell you if it's trending or not.

One thing to remember when you are searching for trending products is that you need to realize that the product can be sustained for an extended period. Make sure that you don't see a product which is like "the fidget spinner," it will only sell for a couple of months. So make sure that you find a product which is trending, and at the same time, can be a long-term product which you can keep selling in your store. With that being said, let's talk about some of the ways to figure out if the product you are about to sell can be a long-term product in your store.

Finding a Long Term Product

One of the best ways to find out if the product is going to be a long-term success for your store; it's to see if the product is a necessity for consumers.

For example, if we look at the supplement industry, many people keep buying supplements as it is a necessity these days. The truth is that many people would like to stay healthy for a long, which is why many people tend to buy a product which will help them stay healthy for a long time.

This is where the supplement industry comes in, and it makes the consumer believe that they have to buy all of these protein powders, which will help them stay young and healthy. The supplement's example would be a great illustration when it comes to making a product a necessity.

Products that people need to buy continuously so that they can live the lifestyle they hope to live is one of the best ways to grow your brand and to bring in more money. For example, if you look at the "fidget spinner," it was not a necessity, but in fact, it was just a trend. To be clear: looking for trendy products is also an essential thing; however, it is not the main thing when it comes to selling a product.

When you're trying to find a winning product in your niche, you need to look at people's necessity and if they will keep buying the product or not. This is why we recommended you start with a subscription-based business platform so that you can keep selling the product to your clients.

Moreover, it is also essential for you to understand that clients are always looking for the next best thing which they can add to their lifestyle. Which means it is your job to make the client believe that they need the product for the rest of their life. That will only happen if the product can deliver continued success in the long-term for the client and can also help them enhance their lifestyle. These two things are imperative when it comes to finding a product that will help you sell and grow your brand. For instance, if you're in the health and fitness niche, it would be an excellent idea for you to find supplements that you can drop ship through private labeling rather than selling your clients a basic t-shirt. Don't get me wrong, you can build a brand based on clothing, as it is a necessity. However, you need to make the client believe that your dress is somehow superior and is of a status symbol.

If you can't find a product that is of necessity, you need to build up a brand where it feels like it is a status symbol to have your clothing or your products. That being said, you need to have some fantastic marketing skills for you to turn the brand into a status symbol.

The skills will come in time, but the main thing you need to figure out is if you are looking to sell a product which will be of necessity or a status symbol.

If you have decided upon finding a product which is of a need, then you are in luck. It will be effortless for you to market it and to grow it into a fantastic brand very quickly. That being said, if you find a product which you can turn into a status symbol, then you are not out of luck. Even though it will take some time, if you're consistent and keep promoting it the way we have taught you, then you will be in a high position to building up a long-term brand that will keep selling.

One thing to keep in mind when finding a status symbol brand is that you need to keep bettering the products you are offering. You have a lot of competition, one selling products off of status symbol, which is why you need to keep beating your competitors by providing better quality products and market better the products. One thing we firmly believe is that marketing's quality. Market your product the right way to the right people, and then you will have no problem finding products that will sell it in your niche.

Make Sure the Ad Copy Is Good

One final thing we would like to talk about is that your advertisement needs to be very good for you to sell the product.

In fact, if he doesn't have great advertising, but you have a great product, then you might be able to sell a couple of units. On the other hand, if you have a terrible product but a great advertisement, you will sell a lot of products. If you can see my point, you need to find a good ad copy for your products. Most of the time, people on AliExpress will provide you with excellent video ads, which you can use and edit for your financial benefits. That being said, you must understand how to find products which are very good in terms of marketability. Now, there are two ways to find a product with great ads, and the first thing would be to ask the AliExpress dealer that they have a good quality ad for the product.

If they don't, then you can record your ad by using your smartphone. Believe it or not, many people don't realize the power of their smartphone. We live in a day and age where we have a fantastic quality camera that will help you to record an excellent ad. That being said, if you find a winning product, but you don't have an ad for it, then you can always create the ad by yourself. Even though it will be a bit more expensive, it will still be in a high position when it comes to being unique with your ads. Ask how convenient AliExpress ads are, many people are probably using the same ad text. This means the best-case scenario for you would be to buy the product and do the ad by yourself. That being said, if you don't have the budget to do that, then you can use AliExpress videos.

Chapter 6:

How to Market Your Business

By now, this book has been through everything regarding dropshipping; from the different types of dropshipping businesses, how to start your own business, to how to pick out the most profitable niche and products.

You see, everything is essential for your business to flourish, but if you can't get people to come into your page/website or to drive traffic to it, then nothing in this book will help you get sales.

It's simple if no one is there to see your product or what you're selling, and then no one is going to buy your products; it is just going to sit there and do nothing. So, to make sales, you need to drive some traffic to your store or page, and that is what we will be talking about in this chapter: how to drive traffic to your store or page.

Learning how to drive traffic can be a challenging task? There is no right or wrong answer. For some people, using websites like Facebook and Instagram could work amazingly, and that is all they do to drive traffic, whereas for others using free traffic techniques could be working beautifully making them some serious sales. So, it is more so of trial and error than getting it right in the first place.

When I started my dropshipping business, I tried everything from Facebook ads to free traffic techniques like creating blogs and sending out e-mails. But all my dropshipping companies work differently. Sometimes one company would work great on getting Facebook traffic, while others might work great on blog traffic or e-mails. So it just depends.

To find what works and what doesn't for you, need to try it out and see for yourself. There is no way to tell if a specific add will generate you millions of dollars or not.

We will talk about the three most significant ways to drive traffic to your product page or website, which would be Facebook ads, Instagram shout outs, and finally, free traffic-utilizing, blogs, e-mails, etc.

Try them all before you stay with one or another as I said before. Some might work well for you compared to the others, so make you try them out ultimately. With all that being said, let us tackle the hardest one first, Facebook.

Drive Traffic With Facebook

Facebook has a lot of users, over 2 billion of them, to be exact. So, there should be a lot of people on Facebook who would be interested in buying your products.

The Facebook advertisement has been used by almost every dropshippers to drive traffic, and this method is probably the cheapest and the most effective way you can use to drive traffic to your product page or store. Now, there are some steps you need to go through before you start advertising your product in the right way utilizing Facebook, which we will be going through this chapter.

First things first, when you create your Facebook ads account, you will need to make sure you add your website pixel on it. This is so important for people using the online dropshipping method.

If you don't add your store pixel onto your Facebook ads account, it will not be able to collect data for your website and products. The pixel will receive things like:

- What kind of people are checking out your product page;
- What kind of people is purchasing your product.

This would equal to a better ad campaign in the future, as you would be able to target specific people to your product page or website.

So, after you have created your Facebook ads account and added your pixel to your Facebook ads account, we can start to advertise your products. Here is what we need to take care before we start advertising on Facebook:

- Finding products like yours
- Finding big companies Facebook ads
- Targeting to a particular age group and country
- Amazing product photos
- Amazing caption
- Split testing

I know there are a lot of things to worry about. However, believe it or not, these are just the basics we need to take care of as there a lot of other advertising methods which can be used; but for now, worry about the basics.

When you start your Facebook ads campaign, it will ask you ad pages or companies related to your niche. What our job is quite simple yet essential.

The first thing we will do is go online and search for our product. For example, if I am selling a car, I will look up "cars for sale, "so I want you to click on all the websites that sell your products. In this hypothetical scenario, I would be clicking through Honda, Toyota, etc., after you do that, I want you to write down all the websites, which are related to your niche or product that you are going to be selling.

After you have all the top websites, I want you to log into Facebook, and I want you to search up the Facebook page's site. Once you have done that, check out if their Facebook likes are over 500,000, and if so, you have found a winner.

You see, what Facebook does with that information on your campaign is that it will promote your product to the specific people on that page. So, let us get back to my hypothetical scenario, if I am selling a car and I add Honda to my targeted Facebook advertisement, then it will specifically target people who are interested in Honda. To sum up:

1. Find a product;
2. Find a Facebook page which has over 500k followers;
3. Advertise the product to the people involved in that page.

Now that you have the keywords and the specific people, you will be advertising your products too, and it is now time to create an eye-catching advertisement.

Since most of you haven't created a Facebook advertisement, I assume, so for you to make sure your notice converts into sales, you will need to make sure your ads look good.

There are a lot of tips and techniques divulged by "supposedly" dropshipping gurus, but some of you may have heard the phrase "if it isn't broke, don't fix it." That means if big companies are successfully advertising their products, you don't need to come up with a different unique way to do it. If you did your research and tried to find big websites or companies specific to your niche, then there is a high chance that you might have seen their Facebook ads pop up. The next time you see it, I want you to examine their advertising and see what kind of video or images they are using.

This will help you build your advertisement, so make sure you review the ads and copy what they are doing, trust me. It will work better if you create a special one.

Now, let's talk about age groups and countries for your advertisements. If you know what your product provides to consumers, you know what kind of people would be interested in purchasing your products.

Before you start your first campaign on Facebook, it will ask you to put an age range on your advertisement. So, if you are going to be selling a car like I am, then you would probably set the age range around 25to 65 as most of the people. Since most 18 years old won't be buying one by themselves and anyone over 65 won't either.

So, our goal is to target it to people who are most likely to buy your product. This takes some research, and there some guesswork involved, but if you specify the age, you will save the right amount of money and get more sales.

Whereas for picking out the county or region to advertise it to. I would recommend you promote it to the U.S.A., only if your budget is small. Most of your buyers will be coming from the United States, so no need to worry about advertising it to any other people.

If you have some spare change left over, you can further your audience to Canada, which could get you more views and get you more sales.

After you have done all of this research is now time to create your advertising image and caption. People don't realize how important it is for you to have the right model and caption for your post. This will either make your post or break it.

So picking out the right photo and caption is important for your advertisement to be a success. How do you pick out the right image for your publication?

Simple, if you did your research correctly looking up for big companies' websites, then you would know the specific type of photo or caption to use, so mimic their advertisement.

Now, after you have decided upon the photos and caption you will be going with, it is now time to add the photo to your campaign. Two things to remember:

- Make sure the picture is high-definition. If it's not high-definition, then it won't stand out from the crowd, and it would also look unprofessional.
- Make sure the photo is compatible on smartphones advertisement, for you to check out what it would look like on a smartphone, click on the smartphone advertisement option it will show you what it looks like.

Now let's talk about the caption, for you to get people clicking on the caption, you need to make sure that it is also eye-catching. You need to make sure you offer your clients with some incentives, like getting this now

81

for 50% off or only 50 in stock. Just like the big companies, you will need to make sure you create urgency by adding an incentive.

Finally, when everything is good to go and ready to be launched you will utilize a tool called split testing. What you have to do is create two similar advertising campaigns with slight changes. For example, one ad could have an age group of 18-50 and the other 25-65.

After the add has been running for some time, it will show you which one works better compared to the other, and this will help you optimize your ad campaigns in the future. This is optional but highly recommended.

That is all for Facebook advertising. Let's now talk about Instagram influencer advertising.

Drive Traffic With Instagram

Instagram is a great place to advertise your products. They have an enormous amount of users and, most of the time; they are more engaging as compared to Facebook.

So, if you are thinking about dismissing the idea of advertising on Instagram, think again as you would be leaving a lot on the table. Note that advertising from

Facebook does go on onto Instagram, but it isn't as potent as it should be.

When you are advertising on Instagram we use a method called "Instagram influencer." It is quite simple:

1. You will find an Instagram page which is related to your topic;
2. You will ask them to promote your product on their Instagram page and finally see the sales come in.

I have used a lot of methods, but this one always works if you want quick deals on your Instagram account use this method.

Now let's talk about the things you need to worry about before you start advertising on Instagram:

- Find the right influencer
- Make sure they don't have any BOTs
- Engagement

So, here is the thing for you. To make sales and rack up some right amount of cash from your purchases, you need to make sure that your influencer would have the right audience. This means you cannot expect to make sales off of a dog bracelet if the page is about "I hate dogs."

Make sure the product you are trying to sell is related to the people who are on that specific page. So, for example, if I want to sell a fishing rod, I would look up: I love fishing promote pages on that.

Before you go out to find your influencer page, you need to make sure that the page has at least 300k followers. If it doesn't, then you are not going to get the engagement you are looking for.

The next thing to take care of would be making sure the influencer you are thinking about working with has a high engagement rate. If people are not tuning in to his/her page, they probably won't see your ads as well.

There are some tools you use to find that out, but if someone is not getting at least 5-10% of their followers like meaning if they have 100k followers and they are not getting at least 5-10k likes, then the chances are the followers are not engaging. This would also show you if the followers are BOTs or not, meaning if they have bought followers or if they are real followers.

Now, let's talk about how to get a shout from these Instagram pages. Message them directly saying you want a shout out. Then once you guys work out a deal ask them for a "story shout out" as those work the best. Ask for a 12-hour story shout out, all the followers will see your advertisement within the 12 hours, so no need to advertise it longer than you should. With that being said, let's now discuss the third method.

Drive Traffic With Blogs and E-mails

This method works great. If someone has already bought from you once and they liked the product or your services, chances are they will buy from you again. Using tools like creating your own blogs or anything of that nature can work well for you to get sales and or to get some traffic into your store. There are a lot of ways you can get free traffic we will only be talking about: the two main ones today would be creating a blog and collecting an e-mail list.

There is a downside to this method. It could take some time to get traffic to your blog and managing the e-mail list, so don't consider this method if you want fast results.

Using blogs and e-mail list to promote your products and services have been used for some time. A lot of successful dropshipping businesses solely use this

85

method for advertising their products and services. So it works, and it works great. Just remember it won't work right away as it takes time.

Now, said that there are four things you need to worry about before you start advertising with this method:

- Create a blog
- Get traffic on the blog
- Collect e-mail subscribers
- E-mail them, not SPAM

So, the first thing you need to do is to create a blog. You will need to create it to start collecting e-mails. How you receive e-mails is quite simple.

Once you have created a blog, I want you to begin publishing about the niche or subject with relates to your store or product. For example, if your online store or your product is regarding fishing, then write a blog about "how to ice fish." Make sure the blog you write is filled with knowledge; people would not want to subscribe to a blog; it is not exciting or providing them with great tricks and tips about the niche.

Once you have created a blog, you will need to start promoting your blog to the right people. This can be done for free. All you have to do is go to Google and search up similar blogs posted in the less 24 hours mark time, go on their blogs comment section and tell every reader to check out your link. It works excellently and equals free traffic.

After you have started to get some traffic into your website, it will be time to collect some e-mails to receive e-mails offer them something.

If your blog and store are related to fitness, offer them a free workout plan if they enter their e-mail. Everyone wants free stuff, so make sure you provide it to them. This should help you collect your e-mail list, and I have personally built up around 10,000 e-mail lists using this technique.

Once you have the right amount of e-mails, you can now start promoting your products, but there is one thing you should not forget: not spam!

People do not like to see e-mail sales every day, so make sure you space it out. Ideally, here is how you should go about e-mailing to your potential client. For the first four days, send them an educational e-mail like "how to fish" or "how to work out," again, something related to your website, and then on the fourth day, you can try to promote your product. This strategy typically works for me, and I am sure that it would work for you. Now, I would like to finish off this chapter. So, please remember that not all of your advertising or ad campaigns will work, some might fail, and some might work and make you a lot of profit, your job is to find out what works for you and what doesn't. Try and make mistakes, this is the answer. If you follow everything I said in this book, you will see success quicker than you had expected.

Also, don't forget to try every method out before you select one because some methods take time and they might work great for you later on, so keep trying. Success will eventually come your way.

Chapter 7:

Free Marketing

In this chapter, we will talk about free marketing strategies, which you can use to make more money with your dropshipping store. As you know, we talked about marketing using paid ads, but now we will talk about marketing strategies that you can use for free to get more sales.

There are many ways that you can go about using this method. One thing I want you to realize is that if you want to see amazing results with your dropshipping store, then it is highly recommended that you use these techniques as a tool instead of your business plan.

To be clear, Facebook ads will always win when it comes to growing a full-term brand, but these free advertising methods will help you to get on your feet without spending a lot of money.

With that being said, there are a lot of strategies you can use to get free marketing, the one thing you have to remember is that it is very time-consuming and will require a lot of your effort to get some return out of it. The gains you will get from this will be not as high as Facebook advertising, but it is free, so there's no complaining about that.

We will be talking about a series of the website which can help you to market for free, but each website and app have a distinctive method.

The leading sites we will be talking about are Instagram, Facebook, blogs related to your niche, and Reddit. That being said, there's a sure way to approach marketing on every single website, we will talk about that you get a better understanding of how you will be getting your sales. Now that we briefly talked about which websites were going to be talking about. Let's start with Instagram.

Instagram

As you know, Instagram is one of the most popular websites or app when we talk about social media. Many of the younger crowd use Instagram, not only to grow their community but to build up their brand.

That being said, there's a specific strategy you need to use to get the right amount of return with your Instagram.

The first thing to remember when you do marketing on Instagram is that you don't want to sound spammy. If you look slimy with your post, then your account will get banned. There is nothing wrong with promoting a product on Instagram. However, you don't want to sell your product non-stop as no one will follow you, and you might get banned.

The first thing you need to do with your Instagram account is to build an audience. The way you're going to grow an audience is by providing them with viral content on your Instagram page. For example, if your niche is based on the health and wellness industry, then it is highly advised that you post viral content about the health and fitness industry. You can post other people's content on your page, make sure that you tag them on your post text.

The second thing you need to do is that you need to be consistent with the post that you're going to be putting up on your Instagram, that means that you will have to post on Instagram at least three times a day. This will help you to build up your account awareness, and you will have a higher reach when you post frequently and volume. Make sure that you post three times a day at least, and use great hashtags for your post.

Also, you need to know that the hashtags have to be related to the position that you're uploading. You can't expect to put up cat hashtags when the post is about health and fitness. You can find hashtags online, and it is straightforward. With every photo or video, add at least 20 hashtags.

Once you have found out the hashtags you are going to be posting, the second thing you need to understand is how the caption looks. You need to make the caption of your post engaging. This means that it needs to have a call to action, for instance, if you are uploading a video of someone deadlifting in the captions, you can write "tag someone who can outlift them." This will get your audience engaging in your post and will get them to tag their friends and families, which will allow you to grow your Instagram page substantially.

Another thing you need to do with your Instagram is that you need to build up your audience very quickly. One of the ways you can do that is by following people on Instagram: to make grow your page, all you need to do is to follow a hundred people who are interested in your niche every day and then unfollow those hundred people the next day. I know it sounds very spammy. However, it works when it comes to growing your Instagram page, and at the end of the day, we are here to grow your business not to make friends. Out of those hundred people, at least 30 people will follow you back every day.

The people that follow you back are you going to be the people you will be marketing your product. One of the ways to get people to buy your products on Instagram is by personally direct message them. You can direct messaging and thanking them for following you, after that, you can link your store in the DM and have a call to action saying that "since you followed this page we will give you a 20% off coupon" this will get people to check out your store and eventually buy.

Soon, you'll have a store that makes $300 a day using this method, so don't think that this method does not work. If you put your time and hustle into it, then you will be in a high position to grow in your store and to getting sales.

Facebook

Not that we have managed to touch upon Instagram, Let's talk about Facebook marketing and how it can help you to grow your page and to get free organic sales. Building your Facebook page is more important than you might think.

The people who like and follow your Facebook and Instagram page will be targeted through your Facebook ads later on in the future. This means that you should be uploading good quality content every day. Same as Instagram goes; you need to keep uploading videos and photos on your Facebook page so that you can attract more audiences and get more likes on your page. Unfortunately, you can't follow and unfollow like Instagram. However, the slow progression of your growth will be excellent as you will get the more engaged audience on your Facebook page.

Another way to grow your Facebook page is by linking your Facebook page on other big Facebook pages that are related to your niche. This allows you to get free traffic and likes on your page. However, you need to do it and in a specific matter, so that people don't think you're spamming. The best way to go about linking your page on Facebook is by writing on the wall of the successful Facebook page saying things like "found this amazing page, thought you might like it" this will give you some traffic to your page, and you might be able to collect some likes.

Once you've got a substantial amount of likes on your Facebook page, you can upload your store on your Facebook page for people who can directly buy your products. Trust me, this method works very well.

Another way to get more sales from your Facebook page, it's the directly post their products on other successful Facebook pages related to your niche. This method will work amazingly and can get you some quick sales. The only thing you need to remember when you are using this method is that you need to make sure that you don't sound spammy. The best way to market your products on Facebook pages for free would be to ride something along the line of, "do you think this product is good?" That way, you look like you generally are interested in this product, and if you want some reviews from people in that specific group. Once you manage to do that, you will have tapped on all the ways you can get sales on your Facebook page.

Blogs

Another way to get sales is by creating something called backlinks on other people's blogs.

The best way to go about this method is to find blogs that are related to your niche and to link your products and the comment section below. Find a blog related to your niche and promoting a similar product; many people write product reviews online on their blog.

What you can do is write in the comment section what do you think about the product that you found, and how it can be better than the product they are writing a review on, or you can also ask for opinions on the product.

The goal here is sound like a third person who stumbled upon your website. This way, you will sound like you are not spamming anybody, and you are looking for real opinions.

One thing to remember is that bloggers will get offended if you keep linking your product, and the chances are that you might not get the returns that you are hoping for at the beginning.

The main thing here is to have enough backlinks so that Google ranks you higher up on the search engine. That way, you will be visible to millions of people from your hard work eventually.

This method is more for the long term gains and can be used with fantastic success if you put in the effort. Impact training backlinks are continued, even once you have the money for Facebook advertisement, make sure that you keep creating backlinks. The best thing you can do for your website is to have your website rank high up in Google. The truth is, Google is a search engine for the internet, and many people go on Google to find products to buy.

Reddit

Now we come on to the final section of the chapter, and perhaps the toughest to crack into.

We will be talking about Reddit and how it can help you to build your brand if done correctly. When it comes to Reddit, the main thing you have to keep in mind is that many people are trolls, and it is tough to promote your product there. However, if you have managed to crack the code, then you will be in a much better position in terms of selling your product the right way, and to see the results that you have been hoping for.

First things first, you need to be engaging on Reddit and not promoting your product all the time. All the people on Reddit can see what you're posting, so if they only see you posting products than they will smell it out and realize like you are indeed the website owner looking to get sales.

You do not want to be in this position, as it will cause you to get banned on Reddit. Self-promotion on Reddit is very taboo, which is why you need to keep engaging and individual communities.

The thing is, when it comes to getting some sales on Reddit, engage a lot for the first three days and, on the fourth day, link your product and ask the community a question about what they think about it.

What you will do is to make you look like you actually care about the community and are here to understand what the product is and if you should get it or not. Your main goal here is to look like a consumer who is ready to purchase the product, in no shape or form you should sound like you own the website. This will get you in deep trouble, and you might as well say goodbye to your account, also when you do post on the page.

Make sure that you are engaged and understanding the comments. If they write bad things about your product, then don't stress. If you fire back, then you will look like someone who is promoting the product, and that's the last thing we want Redditors to think.

Secondly, make sure that you don't do it often and that you are doing it consistently. Use the following method to promote on Reddit, engage fully for the first three days, and on the fourth day, link your product with a question. Repeat the cycle again and again, and you will see some good results from your endeavors.

Make a Plan

Now that you know all the tricks, the tips on how to grow your awareness, and how to get more sales without spending a dime, let's talk about some of the ways you can go about selling more products and to be consistent with this method.

The main thing with following all these methods that we have listed is that you need to be compatible with all of these. This means that you cannot take a day off, make sure that you come up with your plan on the days and time you will be promoting your product on social media. When I was doing this method, it took me about two to three hours to do all of these tactics. So make sure that you spare at least that time throughout your whole day to do a promotion. The great thing about following these steps is that it will yield you both short-term and long-term benefits, so make sure that you are consistent with all the posts.

If you don't have money to advertise, this is your only way out, and you will have to hustle a little bit to see results. We even recommend that you continue with this method once you have some money to advertise, as it will still yield you some fantastic results.

That being said, the final thing you need to do before you start this plan is to sit down and write down all the hours you will be promoting on Instagram, Facebook, blogs, Reddit.

Making a plan is very important when it comes to growing your dropshipping business, especially when you're trying to Market without any money. That being said we come to the conclusion of the chapter, don't think that this chapter is not essential as it can be an excellent tool for your brand if done correctly and the way explained to you in this book. If you want sales for free, this is the answer for you.

Chapter 8:

How to Brand Your Business

One of the most important things when starting your dropshipping store is to brand it, which is exactly what we are going to be talking about now. In this chapter, we will teach you how to brand your dropshipping store the correct way. More specifically, we will also show you how to make it legal, and so you have no issues with the law.

That thing said, let's talk about why it is so vital to brand your store when it comes to dropshipping.

When it comes to dropshipping, you must brand your store, the reason why you need to brand your store is that you need to look legitimate. Many people don't realize this, but consumers are astute. If a store is simply a dropshipping store, they may think they will be scammed. Unfortunately, many people have had bad experiences with dropshipping stores. So, the last thing you want to do is be one of those experiences, which is why it is essential that you brand your store, and you make it look legitimate.

There are many ways to make your store look legitimate, but one of the main things you need to focus on when building your brand with dropshipping is to make your store look neat.

One of the ways to make your store look elegant is by having the right theme. If you're using Shopify, then we recommend either the Debut theme or the Brooklyn theme. These two themes make your store look professional and look and business-oriented.

Moreover, studying other stores can help you tremendously when it comes to building your brand. Your goal should be looking at another source which already has well-established brands, and try to mimic that.

Many people don't realize that but, top stores like Nike and Adidas still study to other stores to grow and improve their businesses. Mind you, these stores are already well-established, but they continue to analyze their competitors.

You should be doing the same. If you want to build a brand, then you need to look at stores that are already doing a pretty good job and take away what you can. However, the main goal for you should be to keep your store looking nice and neat. This means that it should not look spammy.

What are the ways to make your store look spammy? Are there unnecessary and unwanted products that are not related to you? As we talked to you before, you need to make sure that your store has relevant products. This means you should not sell products that are not related to your niche, so if you have any products which are not associated with a niche, then we advise that you get rid of it as soon as possible.

Another thing to note when starting your dropshipping store is that you need to get free of unwanted trust badges. Many people use trust badges to build up their awareness and to make customers feel safe. However, there is important to have a trust badge. It is not advised to have them frequently popping up every 2-3 seconds. Many people overdo or go overboard with the trust badges, and your goal is to have a nice concise trust badge that proves your point and still goes along with the floor at the store.

How many people are using trust badges, which look very neat? One of the stores you should be studying when it comes to building up your brand and to make it look neat is https://www.gymshark.com/

They do a great job when it comes to building-up trust badges and to make it look elegant and concise. This store would be an excellent idea for you to study. As a matter of fact, they started as drop shippers as well, so that should give you the motivation to start your own business that way.

Once you've understood this, we will now talk about how to make your store officially a brand are using some of the tactics that we are going to be discussing.

Logo

When it comes to building up a brand, you need to have a logo. If you don't have a logo, then chances are you will not be successful with your dropshipping endeavors. Having a logo is very important.

There are many ways for you to get a logo, but one of the best ways to get a logo is to hire people online to make it for you.

If you have the money, then this is the best-case scenario: go on https://www.fiverr.com/ and look for people who are willing to build up logos for you.

What they will do is look at your site and come up with ideas for your logo. You studied them, you can either go with the logo or ask them to provide you with all the watermarks you need.

However, if you don't like the logo, you can invite them to revise it and talk about what you are looking for. The more open you are with your designer, the better idea they will have when it comes for making your logo.

That being said, if you don't have the money to hire someone to write up your logo, you can make it by yourself. Many people use canva.com.

This website will teach you how not only to make your logo, but do it quickly and easily. However, the logo will not be as professional as if you paid for it. But it will get the job done when it comes to building up your logo and awareness of your brand.

Once you manage to do that, you will have a better look at your website, and more accurately, you will have more visitors and more people converting to sales. This is why it is essential for you to have to write a logo for your dropshipping store. Naturally, if you already know graphic designing and you will be in a much better position for creating your logo without spending a lot of money.

That being said, whichever way you decide how you'll make your logo, you must know how to build up a logo, and more specifically, that you have a logo for your brand.

Do whatever you can to come up with a logo, and have a logo as soon as possible on your website to make it look professional.

Social Media Is Your Resume

As much as we love social media, something you need to understand when building up your brand is that you need to use social media as your resume when it comes to visibility.

Many people don't realize it, but the main thing that sells a brand is their social media. You need to upload

HD photos and concise images when it comes to building up your brand.

What I mean by that is you need to make your social media look as pretty as possible and as related to your store as possible. Whenever you're posting photos and pictures on social media, have a goal behind it. If you don't have a purpose behind it, chances are your social media will look like every other dropshipping social media. You need to make sure that yours looks good and to the point.

Another thing to make sure is that you need to be on all social media as possible. Not just Instagram, but every social media platform that you can think of you need to be on there. This will not only give you the visibility, but it will provide you with the brand awareness that you're looking for.

Having brand awareness is just as important as building a brand, which is why we highly recommend that you get on as many social media platforms as possible so that you can attract as many people as possible.

With that being said, another thing to make sure when building up your social media is that you need to post regularly. We talked about it previously, but three times a day on Instagram can be a great idea when it comes to building up your social media. Always remember, social media is your resume, so make sure you make it look as pretty as possible. You can also post customer photos if they let you, always ask for consent when posting pictures of your customer as some might not like it.

This will give you the notoriety that you have been looking for when it comes to building up your brand, and also this will make your store look outstanding and help you get more sales.

How to Create an LLC

Now that you understand all the basics of building a brand, let's talk about the most important topic, which is how to make your business LLC.

LLC stands for "Limited Liability Company." Your goal is to create an LLC as soon as possible, so you can avoid any lawsuits against you. This is very important when it comes to building up your brand. Not only does it make you look more legit, but it also helps you to build up a safety net to not only pay a lot less tax but also to avoid any lawsuits.

Starting up an LLC is very easy, and anyone can do it. How many people believe that you have to get your LLC done in different states, but the truth is that you can get it done in any state possible it is precisely the same. Go on Google and look up "how to create an LLC."Once you have figured out how to turn your company into an LLC in your state or country, you will have a great financial tool to improve your business and create your passive income. Start an LLC in your country will be just as easy as LLC in Arizona or Nevada. The LLC will also help you to copyright your company.

Following this advice is very important when it comes to building a brand, which is why you need to fully understand this chapter and follow it because it comes to making your brand legitimate. So, you can start making not only thousands but millions in the future.

To sum up, make sure that you build up a logo that will help you to build that brand awareness. Also, make sure that you don't slack on your social media, as it is essential to use social media as your online resume. Finally, make sure that you use all these topics and all these discussions that we went through in this chapter to create your LLC company.

The importance of balancing your company is crucial so that you can avoid any lawsuits. As I said, it is straightforward to start an LLC company, so I highly recommend creating your LLC company where you live. Doing this in other states will not help you to save money on tax. It is a myth.

One final thing to talk about when it comes to building up a brand is that you need to make sure that your brand looks very neat.

You must spend some time on making your store look elegant and as minimal as possible.

We have given you some websites to look up in this chapter. So make sure that you use those websites to, not only get a better understanding of how to make your website look more professional, but also to see what kind of products they are selling.

Understanding the right marketability, also the products are essential when it comes to building up a legitimate brand. We will not discuss it in this chapter, as we have discussed it in the previous sections on how to find the right product.

That being said, I hope this chapter was helpful to you when it comes to making your brand more professional and to make it legal.

Chapter 9:

Dealing With Problems

In this chapter, we will talk about how to take care of the backend stuff when you are starting your dropshipping business.

One thing you have to remember when you are starting up your dropshipping store is that you need to have an excellent back end for you to be successful and to build-up a brand. Now, there are many ways to about this.

However, we will talk about all the main concerns which need to be taken care of for you to have a successful business. Having an excellent customer service will not only help you to build up your notoriety, but it will also help you to come up with a better plan.

Customer Service

One of the most important things to care about would be to have a rock reliable customer service.

Many consumers have issues with drop-shippers. The problem is that many people don't give them a refund, let alone e-mail them back. To be very successful in this business, it is essential that you don't only take care of the matter at hand, but you also respond very quickly. This will give you fantastic ratings and will get more people to recommend you.

That being said, you don't need to be very helpful, which means giving a refund all the time. If the customer has real issues such as size doesn't fit if they got the wrong order, you can replace it. However, if the customer asks for a refund after six months of getting their order, they probably don't deserve a refund.

Making sure you understand this concept is essential. This will help you to be successful in your endeavors when it comes to growing your business.

Finally, we would also like to tell you that having a well-written refund policy is vital to have uploaded to your store. Also, you need to follow what you say in the refund policy.

You can find millions of significant refund policies online. In fact, if you work on Shopify, they will provide you with a pre-written return policy.

Overall, understanding customer service and the concept behind it is essential. Take your time creating your refund policy, and make sure to stick with, it doesn't matter what happens. However, don't make the refund policy very lenient and always reply to emails if you want to grow your brand. Now that you have a great idea of customer service, let's talk about how to find the right team for your dropshipping business.

How to Hire a Team

One of the most important things to talk about when it comes to building up a dropshipping store is the team. You need to have a productive team, but also you need one who knows exactly what they are doing. This means you can't have a team which is insubordinate and is also very lazy. The best way to hire a worker without spending a lot of money is by looking up on fiverr.com, one of the best websites when it comes to finding cheap reliable employees.

You can also look at https://www.upwork.com/, but I feel like it is costly nowadays. Once you have managed to find people who are going to be a part of your team, make sure that you only pay them based on the work that they do and not hourly. You will lose a lot of money if you start paying them regularly, so make sure that you don't do that.

Another thing is you need to understand what the team is supposed to do for you. You can hire teams to not only fulfill your order but also to do many other things such as replying to e-mails and writing good descriptions for your product. If you want a team to make your life easier, you can hire people to fulfill your orders.

This will make it very easy for you, as most of the time is gone fulfilling orders, especially when you have a lot of orders coming in every day.

There are certain websites that makes it for you automatically, such as https://www.oberlo.com/, but there's a price for that. With that being said, you should look at hiring people to grow your team and to make your business run as smoothly as possible. Don't forget that you need to build up a brand, and the only way you are going to do that is by having a team.

In the beginning, you might not need a group as it is simple to manage since you won't have a lot of orders. However, once you start growing and scaling up your business, it will be very crucial that you pulled the trigger on building up a team.

Make sure that you look for people who not only have good reviews on Fiverr but someone you can trust.

It is totally fine to interview them before you give them the job. You can do an interview on Skype, or maybe even do a phone interview, whether it works.

As long as you know who you're working with and that you can see working with us for a long time, then you will be in a great position to either hire them or fire them based on your needs.

However, don't make the mistake of hiring people who don't know what they are doing. Have general questions for them to answer, and see if they fit the culture. Making sure that they understand the brand and the message behind it is very important. If an employer does not understand that, then you shouldn't hire them. However, it is your job to help them know what the brand entails and why it is so. You need to be very clear with them, as they need to be very clear with you when it comes to job and their responsibilities.

That being said, the leading players in your team should be:

1. Someone who fulfills the orders for you;
2. Someone who does customer service for you;
3. Someone who finds and researches products for you.

All of these employees should be hired once you have managed to scale up your business to a profitable level, and once you can hire them. Don't start hiring people in building up a team once you haven't even scaled them up. So, make sure you have some information base before you hire a team.

Now that we have taken some time to look into dropshipping and how to start your own business, it is time to take a look at a few tips that you can follow to get the most of this business model. Dropshipping is a simple idea, but it does take some work to get things up and to run.

Other Tips

Some of the tips that you can follow to make your business as successful as possible include the following:

- **Focus on your marketing**

    When you get started with your own dropshipping company, you have to take some time to focus on marketing. Even if you plan to list on Amazon or eBay, you still have to spend some time marketing your products to stand out from the crowd.

    There are many sellers and dropshippers out there who are trying to compete for the same market as you. If you don't take the time to market your products and your page, you will end up getting lost in the crowd and won't make any sales.

    We talked about a lot of different ways that you can market your products, and as a business owner, you must learn about how each one can help you grow and scale your own business.

You may find that SEO is the best choice for you, especially if you do your website to sell the products. You may find that spending some time on social media is a better option.

Many new companies like to work with e-mail marketing to see their results show with previous customers.

All of the methods can work well. But if you can think of a new method, one that has you go outside the box, rather than just using traditional methods, then consider that one.

Dropshipping is an industry that has a lot of competition. Finding ways to stand out from the crowd can make a big difference in how successful you will be.

- **Do not underprice your products**

We have talked about this one a little bit, but you have to be careful about the pricing that you have with your products.

Some drop shippers will try to beat out the competition by lowering the prices of their products quite a bit. They think this is a surefire way to convince customers to work with them.

While this may seem like a good idea, and some customers do like to look for a good deal, it can backfire on you on occasion. Many customers know the price of other products, or they know how to search online and compare.

If they see that the price you are listing at is too low, then they will be wary and assume that they are going to get a substandard product and won't want. In this case, you won't be able to make many sales in the process. At the same time, you won't be able to earn as much income in the process either.

The Lower you make the price, the less profit you can make on that item. If you price it too low, the shipping costs and other costs will take up any profit that you make, and it is possible that you would owe money instead of making any money if you aren't careful.

- **Pick a product that makes a good profit margin**

There are a lot of dropshipping products that you can choose from when starting your new business. But you need to make sure that you go

119

with products that are going to earn you a good deal of profit in the process. If you are only going to earn $1 on each product, then it is probably not a good option to go with. You would have to sell thousands of those each month to make any profit at all on them.

The higher the profit margin on the item, the better it is going to be for your business. You can sell a good deal of the items, and make a ton more money in the process. Finding products that make at least a 45% margin after you pay for shipping and taxes can be great as well. If you find products where you can make a profit of $100 or more, that is even better.

How do you make sure that you are finding products that will make you a good amount of profit? First, go through your supplier's pages and decide which products you are the most interested in. Then you can take a look at how much each of those products costs for you to purchase them from the supplier. With that number in mind, go online and see how much other suppliers are charging for that same item.

The last step is important because you want to make sure that your products are priced competitively. You want to get the most out of the pricing, but you also need to be careful not to price too high compared to the competitors.

If you look at the price that the supplier is charging and compare it to the other prices and you see the profit margin is too low, then it is time to move on to a different product. Take your time and search around until you find the right products that will make you enough money to make the process worth your time.

- **Find ways to bundle items together**

As a dropshipper, it is your job to find ways that make your business stand out from the others.

One way that you can do this is to bundle together some of the items that you are selling. This can be beneficial for your customer and for you. Many customers want their shopping experience to be as pleasant and quick as possible. They don't want to spend hours looking for items online that go together or will work together.

If you are able to provide them with a bundle of the items they need in one spot, and if you can even provide it with a little bit of a discount, they are more likely to make that purchase.

This method is going to benefit you, as well. When you get the customer to purchase the bundle, it means a bigger sale for you.

The ideal would be to find a way to turn it into a subscription service, where the customer will purchase the same bundle or product each month so you can keep earning the same income from it over and over again.

- **Pick the right platform that you like the best**

  In previous chapters, we spent some time talking about a lot of different platforms that you can use to start this kind of business. Each one has benefits and limitations that you are going to be faced with, and it is up to you to choose which one seems the best for your needs.

  Some of the bigger sites, like Amazon, Shopify, and eBay can be nice because they already have a lot of name recognition that goes with them. You will already find a lot of customers to work with there. But some benefits come with working on your website to sell products. You get more choices with the templates that you want to use, and you get the benefit of more options with how the website works. And, in the long run, these personal websites often end up being cheaper to use and maintain compared to the other options.

- **Always provide the best customer service**
Customer service is always important, and it is definitely something that you need to pay attention to when it comes to selling your dropshipping products.

There is going to be a ton of competition out there, and one of the ways that you can make yourself stand out from the crowd is to provide the customers with the best service possible. There are many different methods that you can choose that will help you to do that.

You can make it easy for the customer to e-mail or contact you and ask any questions that they may have.

You can bundle your products and services together to make things easier and even cheaper for your customers.

In some cases, sending along a little gift, a personalized note, or even some other special offer can help to provide great customer service that they are going to appreciate and will keep them coming back later on.

Order the product before selling it; this can be a great method to get the same experience that your customer will need when they order from you. It is also a good way to ensure that you are picking out the right supplier for your needs. If you have to go through the whole process just like your customers do, then you will see where the issues can be, and you can decide if that supplier is the right one for you, or if you need to pick out someone else.

To do this process, simply go to the supplier page and order one or more of their products, the ones that you should like to sell to the customer. Fill in all the information and choose the shipping options that you will provide to your customers. Then sit back and wait.

When the product comes, note how long it took and whether or not that time frame is within the amount the company had promised. Take a look at the packaging and how professional it looks. Open the box and look at the product, determining if it is the right product, if it is made out of high-quality materials, and more.

Basically, you want to consider whether or not you would be happy with this product and its speed of delivery if you had purchased and wanted this item for yourself.

If you are considering working with a few different suppliers, then it is best to do these steps with each one. If you want to see which company is better than the other when it comes to similar products, order at the same time from them and see what happens.

You can compare shipping prices, shipping time, the price of the item, and the quality of the item when it gets to you. If you find that there are any issues with the company you want to work with, then it may be best to pick out a different supplier. Don't assume that it is just a one-time thing that happened. You are the face of your business, and if a supplier isn't able to provide a good service and impress your customers, then you are going to be the one who is blamed.

If there are any problems, consider working with someone else to ensure you give the best customer experience to anyone who purchases from you. Starting your dropshipping business can be an exciting time. You have to figure out which products you would like to sell, which supplier is the best one to work with and make sure that you are pricing and marketing the items, so your customers can find them.

When you are ready to get started with this new business model, make sure to check out these tips to make it a little bit easier to work with.

Conclusion

Thank you so much for downloading the book *Dropshipping e-commerce business: a step by step guide for beginners who want to make money online selling on Amazon FBA, Shopify and eBay. Create your passive income and find your financial freedom.*

As you can see, we learned a lot in this book. Not only did we teach you how to start your Shopify or Drop Shipping business. But we also showed you how to scale it appropriately, so that you can build a brand. We spoke about the importance of building up a brand. By now, you should know why it is essential for you to create a brand when starting a dropshipping business.

Moreover, understanding free strategies on how to market is also very crucial. That being said, now you should have all the tools regarding growing your business the right way without losing money. Most of the time, people start dropshipping, without having a clear idea of how to go about it. Unfortunately, many people give them misinformation, and they start losing money. Thanks to this book, you will have all the tools you need to grow your brand and start making a good chunk of change.

So, what's the next step?

Take the time to set up your expectations for this business. While we all dream about hitting a home run on the first pitch, it is worth setting up realistic expectations. Take the time to learn about your local market. Perhaps you can find information on sales and turnover in your area. This will help you get an idea of how big the pie is. At first, getting a sliver of that pie may prove to be a challenge. But keep in mind that any profitable business has a snowball effect, that is, once you get rolling, the ball keeps getting bigger and bigger. Once you have learned the rope, you will find that you begin to spot areas for improvement and ways in which you can better serve your customers. In such cases, you will be able to make the most of your opportunity in the business world. You will gain valuable experience that will lead you to become a serious business person. Who knows, perhaps this is just the beginning of your new career in the business world.

But please bear in mind that there are bumps along the way. Unfortunately, we all make mistakes. As such, we must learn from those mistakes. Negative experiences, while frustrating, can serve to improve the overall functioning of the business. This can lead to bigger and better opportunities at some point down the road. In fact, many of the world's most renowned business leaders hit a few bumps on their way to success.

As you gain more and more experience, running a drop shipping business becomes second nature. You will then know all of the ins and outs. This will enable you to tweak your performance to better suit your particular market and customers. Innovators in the business world always have a leg up on the rest. That is where true fortunes are made. When you are able to innovate in your specific business, you have the potential to become truly special.

That being said, if you enjoyed this book, then we would appreciate it if you can recommend it to your family or friends who are looking to build up their business. We know how hard it is to come up with useful information, which is why we should do that one good deed and tell your friends and family about this book. Also, if there is any part of this book that is not entirely clear, we would highly recommend that you reread the section which you feel you need to brush up on so and you can have a better comprehension of everything that we have presented to you. Sometimes it can be hard to learn it on the first try, which is why we recommend you keep reading this book until you understand every single topic.

As always, keeping a positive attitude is the most important factor to achieve success in anything you do. By keeping a positive mindset, you will be able to overcome any difficulties which may come along your way. Please keep in mind that you have everything you need to become successful. Others like you have been successful. As a matter of fact, all of those who have achieved true success in life have had one very important thing in common: resiliency. They don't back down from a challenge. And when they get knocked down, they get back up and keep moving.

Thank you very much for your attention. We hope that this book has been both useful and informative. Great care went into producing this volume. We sincerely hope it has been useful in getting your new dropshipping business off the ground. See you on the flipside!

www.ingramcontent.com/pod-product-compliance
Lightning Source LLC
Chambersburg PA
CBHW070351220526
45467CB00001B/335